Dump Dinners Box SET 3 IN 1

97 Easy, Delicious and Healthy Dump Dinner Recipes

Table of content

Pamela Bolton

31 QUICK, EASY AND DELICIOUS DUMP DINNER RECIPES

FOR EACH DAY OF MONTH!

DUMP DINNERS

Dump Dinners

31 Quick, Easy, and Delicious Dump Dinner Recipes One for Each Day of the Month!

Introduction

I first want to thank you and congratulate you on downloading this book "Dump Dinners: 31 Quick, Easy, and Delicious Dump Dinner Recipes for Each Day of the Month!" You are really going to enjoy using these 'dump dinner' recipes especially on those extra hectic days when you have to drop your kids off at their different after school activities or clubs that they are involved with. Having a 'dump dinner' on those extra busy days is going to make it that much easier for you to make it through the day.

By making use of this wonderful collection of 'dump dinner' recipes you will take some stress off yourself in not having to worry about preparing a meal on the nights that you are having a 'dump dinner' night. Just imagine how nice it is going to feel for you when you walk through the door after a long day at work to be greeted by the wonderful aroma of your dinner, cooked, and ready to be eaten. I guarantee you this will be a moment that you are going to want more of that is why I have a whole month of recipe collected in this book.

I can tell you from my own experience that the first time I came home to the wonderful aroma of my pot of beef stew, I never turned back. I just love making 'dump dinners' and my family loves them for their taste, so for me it was a win win on making 'dump dinners' part of my families weekly dinners. I feel good that I am providing my family with home cooked meals instead of running my kids to the closest fast food restaurant. Choosing to cook 'dump dinners' is still giving my family good home cooked meals, not only are these healthier but they are much cheaper than eating out. I hope you and your family will enjoy these recipes as much as my family and myself do.

Chapter 1 – What is Dump Dinners?

In this book is a great 31 day collection of 'Dump dinners' for you to enjoy! Dump dinners are basically dinners that are prepared in slow cookers, crock pots or casserole dishes. You don't have to do much in terms of preparation you put all that is needed into the crock pot and turn it on and allow it to cook for eight hours. This is great when you are a busy person living a busy full life with work and family commitments one of them being preparing the family meals. To make this a bit easier for you there is the choice of doing a 'dump dinner', this can cook throughout the day when you are at work so when you and your family arrive home there is a home cooked meal ready and waiting to be served.

Many of us have very busy schedules between our work and home life it can be very stressful and challenging at times in trying to provide a good healthy meal for our family while trying to get other things accomplished at the same time. Often people will be so rushed they will resort to fast food options because they just don't have time or are just too tired to cook a family meal. This is those days when we might go out to a fast food restaurant or perhaps order fast food such as pizza delivered to the house. These choices are much more expensive than choosing to go with the 'dump dinner' option. With the 'dump dinner' option you know that the food that you will be having is a good home cooked meal.

It is a really good idea to try and incorporate 'dump dinners' into your weekly eating plan rather than spending too much money on eating out or ordering in. If you are trying to cut back on expenses then eating out should be one of those expenses that you cut out or at least limit to once or twice a month rather than a couple of times a week. You will feel better in knowing that your kids are eating a proper home cooked meal that will provide them with the nutrients they need to stay healthy and strong. At the same time this will give you a bit of a break in that you do not have to come home from one job to start another job. This will give you the enjoyment of just being able to come home and eat right away sitting down to a meal with your family that you can all enjoy together.

Just by making some planning ahead of time you can feel relaxed in knowing that you do not have to rush home and start peeling potatoes, cutting up meat, and slicing up veggies for the evening meal. Instead you are coming home to a meal that is ready and waiting to be served. You just put the ingredients in the pot, and turned it on before you went to work and the crock pot did the rest.

Well it is time to get your crock pot out and get ready to make some wonderful 'dump dinners' for you and your loved ones. Sit back and smell that roast cooking in your slow cooker on 'dump dinner' night!

Chapter 2 – Dump Dinner Recipes 1-5

1. Chicken Casserole Cantonese Style

Ingredients:

- two cans of unsweetened pineapple chunks, in juice
- one yellow onion, peeled, and sliced
- one teaspoon of garlic, minced
- one teaspoon of ginger, fresh, minced
- two pounds of chicken, skinless, boneless, sliced one quarter of an inch strips
- one cup of low-sodium chicken broth or veggie broth
- two red peppers, sliced into strips
- one can of water chestnuts, drained
- four green onions, sliced
- salt and pepper to taste
- one quarter cup of coconut flour
- one tablespoon of apple cider vinegar
- three tablespoons of soy sauce, reduced

Directions:

Mix garlic, ginger, salt, pepper, and breast strips in the slow cooker, then add pineapple, onion, soya sauce, broth, and water chestnuts.

Cook in slow cooker for six hours. Combine flour with a little water and mix into a paste, stir in to thicken. Serve on top of bed of steamed rice and garnish with chopped onion.

2. Chicken & Mushroom Sauce

Ingredients:

- one broiler chicken, cut into pieces
- four ounces of fresh mushrooms, sliced
- one quarter cup of dry white wine
- one can of mushroom soup

Directions:

Season your chicken with salt and pepper. Place into the crock pot. Mix the wine and soup and pour over the chicken. Pour mushrooms over the top of chicken and cook on low for eight hours.

3. Brisket Dinner

Ingredients:

- six carrots cut into cut into one quarter
- one pound of small boiling onions, peeled
- half a teaspoon of thyme
- one bay leaf
- two teaspoons of salt
- one large carrot, chopped
- one large onion, chopped
- five pounds of beef brisket, well trimmed

Directions:

Cut the brisket in half and place into crock pot. Add carrots, onions, salt bay leaf, thyme, and water. Cook for ten hours covered. Remove the meat keep warm. Add sliced carrot and small onions to pot cook on high for two hours. Remove veggies from pot and place around meat.

4. Meat Loaf & Potatoes

Ingredients:

- one teaspoon of freshly ground pepper
- one teaspoon of salt
- one teaspoon of mixed herbs
- half a cup of finely chopped celery
- half a cup of lengthwise sliced bell pepper
- one cup of no salt tomato juice
- one small onion, chopped finely
- one cup of bread crumbs
- one egg, whisked
- two pounds of ground beef
- one and half cups of ketchup
- half a teaspoon of thyme, chopped

Directions:

Mix all of the ingredients together using your hands except the slices of pepper and ketchup. Shape into a meatloaf and put into greased crock pot. Add ketchup and peppers on top of meatloaf. Cook for eight hours on low

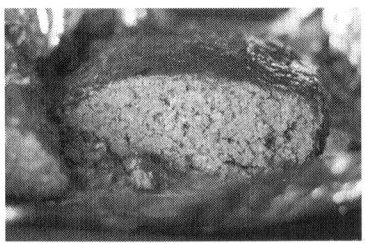

5. Beans & Beef

Ingredients:

- half a cup of bacon, cooked crumbled
- one can of pork and beans
- one 15 ounce can of butter beans, drained
- one 15 ounce can of kidney beans, drained
- half a cup of water
- one third cup of brown sugar
- one and a half cups of barbeque sauce
- half a cup of chopped onion
- half a pound of ground chuck

Directions:

In a slow cooker combine meat, barbeque sauce, onion, brown sugar, water and mix well. Stir in the remaining ingredients, cover cook on low for six hours.

Chapter 3 – Dump Dinner Recipes 6-10

6. Chicken & Rice

Ingredients:

- 12 ounces of long-grain converted rice mix with seasoning
- two cups of broccoli, florets
- one medium sized yellow onion, chopped
- one can of condensed broccoli soup, four ounce can
- one and a half pounds of chicken breasts, cut into cubes
- two and a half cups of water
- two cups of sharp cheddar, shredded

Directions:

In slow cooker, combine chicken, soup, onion, water and mix well. Cover and cook for four hours on low. Add broccoli and rice, cover and cook for another three hours, then stir in cheese and serve.

7. Pot Roast

Ingredients:

- ten ounces of ketchup
- one tablespoon of oregano
- two tablespoons of flour
- two zucchinis, chopped into one inch pieces
- one cup of water
- one ounce of Italian herb mix
- one eight ounce can of Italian tomatoes, pureed, undrained
- two onions, peeled and sliced
- six cups of button mushrooms, sliced
- three pound top roast
- one teaspoon of garlic, minced

Sauce:

Remove and skim fat from slow cooker. Blend water and flour in a small sauce pan until you have a paste, then add juices in slow cooker to it and blend. Cook on high the sauce has thickened. Add the roast back into the slow cooker. Pour sauce over the roast and cook on high until the roast is hot again.

Directions:

Layer your onions and mushrooms on the bottom of slow cooker, add the roast. Sprinkle the Italian herbs over the meat with sauce mix and crushed red pepper. Mix the tomatoes with garlic and oregano and pour over the roast. Add zucchini. Cook on high for five hours, check to see if the roast is tender then remove it from the slow cooker and keep warm.

8. Tuna Casserole

Ingredients:

- two five ounce cans of tuna, drained
- one ten ounce can of cream of celery soup, condensed
- one ten ounce can of cream of mushroom soup, condensed
- eight ounces of fresh cut vegetables of your choice, I use chopped celery (3 stalks) and one red onion, diced, half a cup of shredded carrot
- one cup of coconut milk
- two tablespoons of melted butter
- salt and pepper to taste
- 16 ounce pack of penne pasta, cooked, drained
- half a cup of parsley, fresh chopped
- garnish with Parmesan cheese

Directions:

Combine all of the ingredients except the butter and Parmesan. Pour the mix into a greased slow cooker. Top with melted butter and cook on low for eight hours. Put into serving bowls and garnish with Parmesan cheese.

9. Pulled Pork Sandwiches

Ingredients:

- eight burger buns

- eighteen ounce bottle of your preferred barbeque sauce

- two pounds of pork tenderloin

- one can of root beer

Directions:

Put your pork into the slow cooker and pour the root beer over the meat. Cook on low for six hours. Remove the pork and shred with forks. Pour in barbeque sauce with shredded meat in pot. Serve on burger buns.

10. Beef Stroganoff Crock Pot Style

Ingredients:

- one packet of egg noodles
- eight ounces of sour cream, light
- two tablespoons of corn starch
- one can of ginger ale
- one ten ounce can of cream of mushroom soup, condensed
- one packet of onion soup mix
- one can of mushrooms, or fresh mushrooms, sliced
- two pounds of stewing beef, sliced into bite size pieces

Directions:

Place your stew meat into the crockpot. Add onion soup mix, mushrooms, soup, and ginger ale. Cook on high for four hours stir occasionally. During the last hour stir in starch with a small amount of water. Add sour cream. Cook the egg noodles according to the package instructions. Serve the Stroganoff over egg noodles.

Chapter 4 – Dump Dinner Recipes 11-15

11. Zucchini & Sausage Soup

Ingredients:

- two cups of vegetable stock
- one cup of tomato sauce
- two cups of water
- one celery stalk, chopped
- one red onion, chopped
- one can of diced tomatoes
- one pound of Italian sausages, sliced
- two tablespoons of olive oil
- one zucchini, cubed
- salt and pepper to taste
- one teaspoon of basil, dried
- one teaspoon of oregano, dried

Directions:

Heat a skillet with oil then put in sausages. Cook on all sides for five minutes then add celery and onion, saute for five minutes. Transfer the mixture to your crockpot and stir in the remaining ingredients. Add salt and pepper to taste and cook on low for five hours.

12. Lentil & Ham Soup

Ingredients:

- one teaspoon of Worcestershire sauce
- salt and pepper to taste
- one teaspoon of hot sauce
- one cup of diced ham
- three celery stalks, diced
- two carrots, diced
- one red onion, chopped
- one teaspoon of coriander seeds
- four cups of low-sodium chicken stock
- two cups of dried lentils, rinsed
- two tablespoons of parsley, dried

Directions:

Combine all the ingredients into your crock pot add salt and pepper to taste and cook on low for five hours.

13. Vegetable Barley Soup

Ingredients:

- two cups of tomato puree
- two cups of dried barley, rinsed
- one yellow pepper, and one red pepper, diced
- one red onion, chopped
- one zucchini, diced
- two tablespoons of olive oil
- two pounds of beef roast, cubed
- salt and pepper to taste
- two cups of vegetable stock
- two cups of water

Directions:

Heat oil in a pan then add beef. Cook for five minutes on all sides until brown then add to crock pot. Add the rest of the ingredients and season to taste with salt and pepper. Cook on high for three hours.

14. Parmesan Meatballs

Ingredients:

- one cup of breadcrumbs
- two tablespoons of parsley, chopped
- two eggs
- one teaspoon of oregano, dried
- one teaspoon of basil, dried
- one cup of almond meal
- one cup of Parmesan, grated
- one pound of ground beef
- one pound of ground pork
- one teaspoon of brown sugar
- one cup of low-sodium beef stock
- two tablespoons of olive oil
- one teaspoon of all-spice powder

Directions:

Combine all of the ingredients in a bowl except the stock and Parmesan. Pour the stock into your crock pot and form meatballs. Place meatballs into crock pot and cook on low for eight hours. Garnish top with Parmesan when done.

15. Spinach Beef Stew

Ingredients:

- one pound of baby spinach, shredded
- one cup of beef stock low-sodium
- salt and pepper to taste
- two shallots, finely chopped
- one teaspoon of chili flakes
- one can of diced tomatoes
- one teaspoon of garlic, minced
- two tablespoons of olive oil
- two pounds of beef roast, cubed

Directions:

Heat oil in pan add the beef and brown then add beef to crock pot. Stir in the tomatoes, garlic, shallots, and beef stock. Add the salt and pepper along with chili flakes. Cook on low for six hours. Stir in the spinach and cook for another 30 minutes.

Chapter 5 – Dump Dinner Recipes 16-20

16. Sesame Chicken

Ingredients:

- one cup of organic honey
- two tablespoons of tomato puree
- one tablespoon of sesame oil
- one teaspoon of garlic, minced
- one shallot, finely chopped
- six chicken thighs
- one cup of cold water
- two tablespoons of soy sauce

Directions:

Place the chicken thighs into your crock pot. Mix the rest of the ingredients in a bowl. Pour over the chicken and cook on low for six hours. Serve chicken warm topped with sesame seeds.

17. Pork Tenderloin Stuffed with Goat Cheese

Ingredients:

- four ounces of goat cheese
- one teaspoon of oregano
- one teaspoon of thyme, dried
- salt and pepper to taste
- one cup of low-sodium chicken stock
- three pounds of pork tenderloin
- one cup of apricots, dried

Directions:

Mix the goat cheese with the apricots, thyme, and oregano. Cut the pork tenderloin in butterfly style so you will be left with a sheet of meat. Put the goat cheese mixture on one end of the pork and roll tightly. Secure with toothpicks and place your pork into the slow cooker. Add stock and salt and pepper cook for eight hours on low. Serve with a favorite side dish of veggies.

18. Peach Glazed Baby Ribs

Ingredients:

- one and a half cups of peach nectar
- one cup of white wine
- one teaspoon of ground black pepper
- one red pepper
- one stick of cinnamon
- four pounds of ribs
- one teaspoon of garlic, minced
- two tablespoons of parsley, fresh, chopped

Directions:

Mix the wine with the peach nectar, garlic, cinnamon, and red pepper in your slow cooker. Season the ribs with salt and pepper and place into slow cooker. Cook on low for eight hours. Serve with a nice simple side dish.

19. Honey Glazed Ham

Ingredients:

- one cup of organic honey
- one tablespoon of orange zest
- one teaspoon of salt
- four tablespoons of Dijon Mustard
- four pound piece of ham
- one teaspoon of cloves, ground
- one cup of light beer
- one teaspoon of chili flakes

Directions:

Mix spices, mustard, and honey then spread over ham. Place ham into slow cooker. Pour beer over and cook on low for eight hours.

20. Asian Chicken Wings

Ingredients:

- one teaspoon of chili flakes
- one cup of soy sauce
- one cup of concentrated orange juice
- one cup of brown sugar
- two teaspoons of garlic, minced
- four pounds of chicken wings
- one teaspoon of sesame oil

Directions:

Mix all ingredients accept wings in a bowl, blend well. Add wings and pour mixture over wings cook on low for eight hours.

Chapter 6- Dump Dinners Recipes 21-25

21. Bell Pepper Stew

Ingredients:

- one can diced tomatoes
- one jar of roasted bell peppers, chopped
- two teaspoons of garlic, minced
- one shallot, chopped
- two tablespoons of olive oil
- one and a half pounds of chicken, skinned, peeled, cubed
- salt and pepper
- one medium red potato, diced
- parsley, chopped for garnish

Directions:

Add all of your ingredients to the slow cooker. Season with salt and pepper and cook on low for four hours.

22. Lamb & Potato Stew

Ingredients:

- one teaspoon of ground ginger
- two tablespoons of olive oil
- one teaspoon of rosemary, dried
- three pounds of lamb shanks, cubed
- four cloves of garlic, chopped
- one teaspoon of cumin seeds
- one and a half pounds of red potatoes, peeled and cubed
- one cup of orange juice
- one tablespoon of orange zest
- one bay leaf
- one and a half cups of vegetable stock
- half cup of parsley, chopped for garnish

Directions:

Heat the oil in a pan add the lamb and stir until all sides are brown. Transfer to your slow cooker then add other ingredients and stir. Add salt and pepper to taste cook on low for eight hours.

23. Beef Carrot Stew

Ingredients:

- two tablespoons of olive oil
- two teaspoons of garlic, minced
- two red onions, sliced
- two pounds of beef roast, cubed
- one bay leaf
- salt and pepper to taste
- one cup of low-sodium beef stock
- one can of tomatoes, diced
- four carrots, sliced
- one piece of celery, chopped, finely
- one cup of cilantro, fresh, chopped for garnish

Directions:

Heat the olive oil in a pan then add beef and brown on all sides. Then, transfer to slow cooker add other ingredients and stir. Season with salt and pepper. Cook stew for eight hours on low. Add to serving bowls when done and top with cilantro.

24. Chicken & Couscous Mediterranean Style

Ingredients:

- one cup of couscous, rinsed
- two tablespoons of olive oil
- two tomatoes sliced
- two cups of chicken stock
- one cup of black olives, pitted, sliced
- two tablespoons of parsley, chopped
- one lemon, sliced
- six chicken thighs

Directions:

Combine the parsley, olive oil, lemon juice, tomatoes, olives, couscous in crock pot. Season with salt and pepper, place chicken on top of couscous. Cook on high setting for three hours.

25. Spicy Ragu

Ingredients:

- three red onions, chopped
- four tablespoons of olive oil
- salt and pepper to taste
- one cup of beef stock
- one cup of tomato sauce
- one can of tomatoes, diced
- two and a half pounds of ground beef
- four cloves of garlic, chopped
- garnish with fresh parsley, chopped and Parmesan, grated

Directions:

Heat the oil in a pan then add the onions and stir. Cook for a few minutes until onion is soft. Stir in beef, and garlic. Cook for an additional few minutes. Transfer to the crock pot and stir in the rest of the ingredients. Cook on low for eight hours. Serve on top of favorite pasta and garnish with parsley and Parmesan.

Chapter 6 – Dump Dinner Recipes 26-31

26. Chicken Shrimp & Tomato Stew

Ingredients:

- one celery stalk, sliced
- one carrot, sliced
- one shallot, chopped
- one and a half pounds of chicken breast, skinned, boned, cubed
- one yellow pepper, cored and sliced, one red pepper, cored and sliced
- one can of tomatoes, diced
- salt and pepper to taste
- one pound of fresh shrimps, peeled and deveined
- two tablespoons of cilantro, fresh, chopped

Directions:

Combine shallot, celery, chicken, peppers, tomatoes, pepper in crock pot. Cook for three and a half hours on high setting. Add the shrimps and cook for an additional 30 minutes on high then sprinkle with cilantro before serving.

27. Crock Pot Jambalaya

Ingredients:

- one teaspoon of garlic, minced
- one onion, chopped
- one red pepper, cored, and diced
- three cups of chicken stock
- one and a half cups of white rice, rinsed
- four Chorizo sausages, sliced
- one pound of chicken breast, skinned, boned, cubed
- two celery stalks, chopped
- one can of tomatoes, diced
- salt and pepper to taste
- one pound of shrimps, peeled, deveined
- two tablespoons of olive oil

Directions:

Heat the olive oil in pan and stir in the onion, garlic, bell pepper, and celery, cook for five minutes. Transfer to the crock pot and stir in the tomatoes, rice, stock, Chorizo sausage, and chicken. Add salt and pepper to taste and cook on low for eight hours. Spread the shrimp over the top of Jambalaya and cook for 30 additional minutes on low setting.

28. Chickpea & Sausage Curry

Ingredients:

- one tablespoon of olive oil
- one shallot, chopped
- four chicken sausages, sliced
- one celery stalk, diced
- two tablespoons of curry paste
- one cup of tomatoes, diced
- one cup of dried chickpeas, rinsed
- one red bell pepper, cored, and diced
- one teaspoon of garlic, minced
- one carrot, diced
- two cups of water
- one cup of coconut milk
- one bay leaf
- salt and pepper to taste

Directions:

Heat the olive oil in a pan and stir in the sausages. Cook for five minutes on all sides, add garlic, and shallot and saute for two mintues. Transfer the mix to crock pot and stir in the rest of the ingredients. Cook on low for eight hours, when done drizzle in the coconut milk. Serve warm.

29. Chicken Noodle Soup

Ingredients:

- one whole chicken cut into smaller pieces
- two carrots, sliced
- eight cups of water
- one celery stalk, sliced
- eight ounces of egg noodles
- one fresh thyme sprig
- one onion, quartered
- salt and pepper to taste
- half cup of parsley, fresh chopped
- one bay leaf

Directions:

Combine the chicken, carrots, water, onion, celery, bay leaf, and thyme in your crock pot. Season with pepper and salt to taste and add parsley mix well. Cook for eight hours then stir in the noodles and cook for an additional 20 minutes on low setting.

30. Ratatouille

Ingredients:

- two tablespoons of parsley, chopped
- salt and pepper to taste
- one teaspoon oregano, dried
- two red bell peppers, cored, and diced
- one yellow bell pepper, cored and diced
- two zucchinis, sliced
- one eggplant, peeled, cubed
- one teaspoon of garlic, minced
- two onions, chopped
- four Roma tomatoes, diced
- one teaspoon of basil, dried

Directions:

Heat oil in a pan add onions, and garlic and saute for a few minutes. Transfer the mix to your crock pot. Add the rest of the ingredients and add salt and pepper to taste. Cook on low for seven hours serve warm or chilled.

31. Split Pea Soup

Ingredients:

- one package of dried split peas, rinsed
- one cup of ham, diced
- one shallot, chopped
- one carrot, diced
- four cups of water
- two cups of chicken broth
- salt and pepper to taste
- one teaspoon of garlic, minced
- one celery stalk, diced
- one teaspoon of basil, dried
- cup of cilantro, fresh, chopped for garnish

Directions:

Combine carrots, shallot, celery, garlic, oregano, basil, ham and split peas in your crock pot. Add the stock and water then season with salt and pepper. Cook on low for six hours. Serve warm topped with cilantro.

Conclusion

I hope that you and your family will be able to have more quality time together when you are cooking these wonderful 'dump dinner recipes up' for you all to feast upon. Learning how to put these great slow cooker meals together is going to give you some free time that you would normally be chained to the stove watching over your meal as you cook it. Well this books recipes will help to break that chain so you are free to do other things that you enjoy!

Time is precious and the more time you can avoid wasting doing mundane things like being chained to a stove, then the more likely your health and well-being will thrive.

Thanks again for downloading my book I would really appreciate if you would be so kind as to leave a quick review on the book—it will be a great help to getting my book viewed by other people out there that want their stove chains broken too!

DUMP
DINNER
—— COOKBOOK ——
FOR BUSY PEOPLE
25 EASY & DELICIOUS DUMP DINNER RECIPES

ANDREA GILLBERT

Dump Dinner Cookbook

25 Amazing Dump Dinner Recipes For Busy People

Table of content

Introduction

Have you heard of this Dump Dinner idea? You may have come across these on Pinterest and it never steers you wrong. Correct? This needs further exploration and research. Now you don't have to follow the recipes religiously because there are those instances when life happens and you have to work with what is available. Even though these are easy to prepare you should still take pride in your work. The memories you want to invoke will have the family eager to gather at the table. No pressure because we are in this together and you do not have to possess superb cooking abilities. You don't have to be perfect but an open mind will help. I also used a few recipes from a cookbook called Tone Your Tummy Type by Denise Austin. I have been focused on using fewer ingredients to cook for a while. I looked for recipes with these qualities. Some are more and I still wanted to create something amazing. It is approached relatively for busy people. This works quickly and without hassle. Here are additional tips for meal preparation:

- Precooked chicken

- Salads are always a good idea

- Homemade soup- I included one for chili soup

- Tomatoes, olive oil, and basil are a quick filling meal

- Baked potatoes and sweet potatoes. You can add cheese, butter or salsa

- Fried Rice- olive oil, chopped onion, scallions, peas, and scrambled eggs to go along with Asian cuisine

Chapter 1 – Seafood

There are some important things to consider about <u>seafood</u> such as safe handling measures. Some family members may be allergic and always look firm shrimp that look firm and have a slight odor. This first one is southern fare. There are variations on the consistency of the sauce. It may be some spice. You can also browse other seafood blogs for ideas.

Yummy Shrimp Creole
- 1 chopped onion

- 1 green pepper

- 1 tablespoon minced garlic

- 2 (15oz) cans fire roasted tomatoes

- 1 T Worcestershire sauce

- 1 pack Sazon Goya

- 1-2 lbs. cooked deveined shrimp

- 1 cup cooked brown rice

Directions

Drizzle olive oil in a pan. Sauté onion, pepper, and garlic over medium heat until tender. Add undrained tomatoes, tomato sauce, sugar, Worcestershire sauce, hot sauce, and crushed red pepper. Simmer for 10 minutes. Stir in shrimp. Cook until heated 1-2 minutes. Serve this over brown rice.

Teriyaki Swordfish - Serves 3

It should have firm flesh. There are three kinds; Pacific, Atlantic and Mediterranean. Easy to make on the grill too and rated as a sustainable seafood choice.

- 3 tsp teriyaki sauce

- 3 tsp sesame oil

- 1 1/2 tsp grated orange peel

- 1 ½ tsp minced garlic

- 3 swordfish steaks

- ½ tsp lemon pepper seasoning

Directions

1. Assemble all ingredients into a freezer bag, Seal and flatten to squeeze out the air. Put into the freezer. When you are ready to make this, thaw in the refrigerator overnight.

2. Preheat oven to 350 degrees. Grease a baking dish with cooking spray and bake for 15 minutes.

3. This goes well with romaine lettuce with carrots and tomatoes along with the dressing of your choosing.

Feel free to add any additional toppings.

Chapter 2 – Soups & Stews

Chili Soup

Other add-ins can be potatoes, tomato juice. Some regions of the United States declare it is not chili without beans. Also, try a splash of hot sauce. Now you will be probably adding meat and this is a dish you want to braise. This means you are simmering meat in a liquid for about an hour until it becomes tender. The majority of cooks add tomatoes towards the end of cooking time.

- 2 roma tomatoes

- 1 can kidney beans

- 1 can black beans

- 1 small Yellow or white onion

- 1 stalk of Celery

- Baby carrots

- ½ tsp chili powder and cumin

- Chicken broth

- ¼ cup Balsamic vinegar

- Parmesan cheese

Directions

1. Put all ingredients into a pot and give it a stir. Bring to a boil and then turn down the heat to low. Simmer for 20 minutes Add water during simmer tine. Allow to cool.

2. Put all ingredients into a freezer bag. Seal tight and mix. Put into the freezer. When you are ready to make this, defrost in the refrigerator.

Beef Stew - Serves 4

Guaranteed to be a win-win situation. I mean imagine the aromas wafting from this prize. Achieving perfection for this <u>dish</u> should be considered a super power. Your sear the meat. Give it a sizzle for at least five minutes.

- 1 pound beef cubes
- 4 sliced carrots
- 4 cubed potatoes
- 1 package dry onion soup mix
- 2 cans 98% fat free can of mushroom soup
- 1(8oz) can of tomato sauce
- 1 (10oz) package frozen peas
- ½ tsp steak sauce

Directions

Put all the ingredients into a freezer bag. Seal the bag after mixing. Put in the freezer. Thaw in the refrigerator a day before slow cooking. Simmer on low heat for 7-10 hours.

Black Bean Taco Soup

You can add other beans such as pinto and kidney. Some other suggestions are ranch dressing and corn. Grated cheese. Mmm. Even though spring is in the air you can still eat this and freeze it for up to six months. Add some cornbread. How many bowls will you eat?

- 1 pound ground turkey

- 1 package mild taco seasoning

- 1 (16 ounce) can black beans rinsed and drained

- 1 (16oz) bag frozen corn

- 2(14 ounce) cans stewed tomatoes

- 1 (8oz) can tomato sauce

- 1 (4oz) can diced green chilies

- 1 pack Sazon Goya w/Coriander and Annatto

Directions

1. Cook meat and onion together. Allow it to cool and then put into a freezer bag.

2. Toss the other ingredients in and mix. Seal the bag. Freeze and 24 hours before you are ready to make this, thaw in the refrigerator. Cook on high heat 1-2 hours or 2-3 ½ hours on low heat.

Additional toppings: tortilla strips, cheese, sour cream, and guacamole.

Hungarian Goulash

The best and genuine kind is made with Hungarian paprika, tomatoes, and green peppers. Every chef usually add their own touch to this dish. Sometimes there are potatoes and noodles. It has a history of being cooked in a cast-iron skillet over an open fire.

Hungarians proclaim it as soup.

- 1/3 cup olive oil

- 3 sliced onions

- 2 T sweet paprika

- 2 tsp salt

- ½ tsp black pepper

- 3 pounds beef stew meat cut into cubes

- 1 (16 ounce) can tomato paste

- ½ cup water

- 1 tsp minced garlic

- 1 tsp. salt

- 1 splash of worcestershire

Directions

1. Drizzle oil in a large saucepan or pot. Sauté onions and stir constantly until softened. Take them out put them on a plate.

2. In a bowl mix paprika, 2 tsp salt and pepper. Douse the beef into this mixture and add to the pot. Brown it on both sides. Add the onions, sugar, and then tomato paste, water, garlic, and the rest of the salt.

3. Turn down the heat. You should the food and allow it to simmer for 1 ½- 2 hours.

Chapter 3 – Classic Meals

God bless <u>Italy</u> for this classic. It is usually served at big parties but that doesn't mean it can't be dinner for your bunch. The weather may not be cold but no reason you cannot enjoy the warmth of these flavors. Serve with some crusty bread or grated Parmigiana or Romano.

Chicken Cacciatore
- 1 pound chicken breasts

- 1 jar of garden vegetable spaghetti sauce

- 1 large diced zucchini

- 1 chopped green pepper

- 1 chopped sweet onion

- ½ tsp seasoned salt

- ½ cup chicken broth

Directions

Transfer these ingredients to a Ziploc freezer bag. Put in the freezer and when ready to cook thaw 24 hours prior. Cook in the crock pot on low setting 6-8 hours. Serve along with linguine and sprinkled with parmesan cheese.

Orange Chicken - Serves 4
This one is much better than takeout. It is a basic <u>recipe</u> that takes the mystery out of what goes into it. I wanted to come up with a hack to do justice to a genuine recipe. You know the difference between moist and greasy and sweet and

saccharine. The ingredients are easy to retrieve. Try to make a marinade of soy sauce and ginger before cooking. Enjoy.

- 3-4 boneless chicken breasts cut into chunks
- ½ tsp cornstarch
- Olive oil
- ½ tsp salt
- 1 tsp balsamic vinegar
- 3 T ketchup
- 6oz orange juice
- 4 teaspoons brown sugar
- 1/3 cup flour
- 1 splash of pineapple juice

Directions

1. In a Ziploc freezer bag combine orange juice, brown sugar, vinegar, salt, cornstarch and ketchup.

2. Pour flour in a plastic bag or plate and douse the chicken with it. Dust off the extra.

3. Drizzle olive oil in a skillet and sauté the chicken. No need to fully cook since it is going in the crock pot. After the chicken has a nice browning, toss it in the crock pot. Pour the sauce mixture over the meat and stir. Cook on low setting for 5-6 hours or 2-3 hours on high. Serve over rice.

Beef Stroganoff

It may be an older recipe but over time it has been refined. In 1891, it claimed first Prize winner of L'Art Culinaire. The early American version adjusted it with Worcestershire sauce and sweet cream instead of sour cream. A salad may be an unusual side dish for this meal but try it. Mustard and Rhine wine can also add flavor.

- 2 pounds sliced beef

- 1 cup sliced mushrooms

- 1 package onion soup

- 1 can cream of mushroom soup

- ¼ cup red wine

- 1-2 T cornstarch

- 1 (8oz) sour cream

- 1 package egg noodles

- ¼ cup water

- ½ tsp Worcestershire sauce

Directions

1. Put meat in crock pot.

2. Next combine mushrooms, cream of mushroom soup, and red wine

3. Simmer on high setting for 2-3 hours or low 4-6 hours stirring occasionally.

4. In the last hour mix the cornstarch with a small amount of water and add to thicken

5. Add sour cream.

6. Boil noodles according to package instructions.

Cold sour cream will curdle in the stroganoff.

Instead of noodles you can serve with thick toast, biscuits, or mashed potatoes.

Oven option:

Preheat oven to 350 degrees and bake for 30-45 minutes.

Once it cools. Transfer it to a freezer bag. Seal tight and flatten to remove the air. Freeze and when you are ready to eat it, defrost in the refrigerator overnight. Reheat in the microwave or the oven.

Lemon Dill Chicken

This is a <u>Greek</u> dish that goes with broccoli or risotto. Other alternatives are wild mushroom over fettucine. You can add honey or chives and used fresh dill. You can also use chicken thighs and drumsticks or a whole fryer chicken. Side dishes can be a mixed green salad or noodles. You can also make a change by putting them on skewers and then the grill. If there are any leftovers use the chicken to make a salad for lunch.

- 4 boneless chicken breasts

- ½ Tablespoon dill seasoning

- ¼ cup extra virgin olive oil

- Juice from half a lemon

- 1-2 Tablespoons minced garlic

- 1 T lemon pepper seasoning

Directions

1. Toss chicken into a large freezer bag. Label the bag with name of recipe and instructions.

2. Combine the remainder of the ingredients in a measuring cup or a bowl.

3. Pour this in the same bag with the chicken.

4, Place in your freezer until it is time to make this.

5. This is best prepared by taking it out of the freezer and putting into the refrigerator the night before. It takes about 6 hours on a low setting.

Chapter 4 – Mexican Cuisine

Chicken Fajitas

Did you know fajita means little belt? Marinate the chicken with jalapenos if you want a bit more spice. You can also use steak. Sear on an iron skillet. You can create your own topping. Some recipes call for chipotle seasoning. It is not necessary but it is always good to experiment.

- 1 pound boneless chicken breasts or cutlets cut into strips

- 2 T olive oil

- 1 sliced medium onion

- 2 large seeded and sliced bell peppers

- La Banderita flour tortillas

- 1 pack of Senora Verde Fajita Seasoning mix

- ¼ cup water

Toppings: cheese, sour cream, guacamole, salsa

Directions

1. Preheat oven to 400 degrees.

2. Grease a skillet and add the chicken strips.

3. Once the meat is no longer pink add fajita mix and water.

4. Stir and allow to cook for 3-5 minutes.

5. Stir in onions, peppers, and transfer to the oven.

6. Bake uncovered 20-25 minutes until chicken and vegetables are done. Spoon onto tortillas.

Mexican Chicken Lasagna

Cumin always pairs well with chicken especially in Mexican cuisine. Lasagna can be tricky but not this version. You can use ricotta cheeses or regular lasagna noodles. There are different varieties with black beans. Another with refried beans or you can use regular ground beef.

- 3-4 cups cooked chicken
- 1 can fiesta nacho cheese
- 1 tsp cumin
- 1 can mild Ro-Tel tomatoes
- ¼ c chopped cilantro
- 4 large burrito tortillas
- 1 cup frozen or canned corn
- 2 cups shredded Mexican Blend Cheese
- A handful of black olives

Toppings; chopped tomatoes, jalapenos, sour cream, lime wedges

Directions

1. Preheat oven to 350 degrees.

2. Stir the following together for the filling: chicken, chicken soup, mushroom soup, nacho cheese, tomatoes, and cilantro.

3. Spread 1 cup of this filling into a casserole dish coated with cooking spray. Start layering with tortillas, corn, beans, then more filling. Filling and cheese should be the top layer.

4. Bake covered loosely with foil but do not let the foil touch the cheese. Bake for 20 minutes then take off the foil and bake 10 more minutes until hot. Put on your toppings.

Shredded Chicken Tacos

Could you eat these every day? Probably and you do not need many ingredients. You know you can also make burritos, or enchiladas with this meat? Other veggies to accompany it; radishes, lettuce, and red onions. Another discovery was grilled scallions.

- 2 ½ pounds chicken breasts

- 1 tsp garlic powder

- 2 tsp onion powder

- ¾ cup chicken broth

- 1 tsp lime juice

- ½ cup Zesty Italian salad dressing

- ½ tsp black pepper

- ½ tsp cayenne pepper

- 1 T chili powder

- 1 tsp paprika

- 1 tsp salt

- 1 tsp cumin

- ½ tsp seasoned salt

Directions

1. Put chicken into the crock pot.

2. Combine the rest of the ingredients in a bowl and whisk vigorously

3. Marinate the chicken with this mixture and cover the crock pot with a lid.

4. Cook chicken on low temperature for 6-8 hours.

5. Start shredding the chicken and then cook it in the broth for another 30 minutes on the same setting.

6. Drain the broth and serve on soft tacos.

Chapter 5 – Comfort Foods

Everyone may not love it, but for those that do will love the effort you put into it. Common mistakes are crunchy vegetables, coarse texture or grease. If you have a food processor you can use it to transform beef to a smooth texture and bake it on a cookie sheet instead of a pan.

Meatloaf

- 1 ½ pound ground chuck
- 1 beaten egg
- ¼ c milk
- 1/2c tsp salt
- ¼ c breadcrumbs
- ½ cup chopped onion
- 2 T chopped green pepper
- 2 T chopped celery
- ½ tsp pepper
- 6 small chopped potatoes

Directions

1. Combine breadcrumbs, eggs, milk, and salt. Wait for it to soften.

2. Stir mixture into meat and vegetables until well blended. Form into a loaf and place into slow cooker.

3. Arrange potatoes around the meat. Cover and cook on high setting for 1 hour or low for 8-9 hours.

Salisbury Steaks

Did you know you can make meatballs out of these? Extra gravy for those potatoes, perhaps? You can achieve restaurant quality after a few tries and experiments such as mustard. Work on making the ideal gravy. This includes onion, beef broth, ketchup, seasoning salt, cornstarch and Worcestershire. Either way this dish will be devoured. Only make this yourself and never settle for the frozen variety.

- 2 pounds lean ground beef

- 1 packet onion soup mix

- ½ cup Italian breadcrumbs

- 1 egg

- ¼ cup milk

- Flour

- 2 cans cream of mushroom soup

- 1 pack au jus mix

Directions

1. Take a large bowl and combine beef, onions, soup mix, breadcrumbs, egg, and mix together.

2. Make 8 patties.

3. Dip the patties into flour.

4. Brown on both sides and after they brown put into slow cooker.

5. While they are cooking, make the au jus concoction according to package instructions.

6. Pour in both cans of soup.

7. Dump this over the patties.

8. Cook on low heat for 4-6 hours.

Blackberry BBQ Chicken

You may want to grill this sauce you prepare yourself. You may never go back to store brand. I sincerely hope you try the thin vinegar based, thick tomato sauce, or mustard based sauce instead of the grocery store brand. Have you heard of Carolina style? Check it out here.

- ¾ cup ketchup

- ¾ cup blackberry jam (another flavor will work too)

- 1/8 cup white vinegar

- 1 tsp chili powder

- 1 1/2 pounds chicken breasts or pieces

- ½ tsp seasoned salt

If you are making this the same night; preheat oven to 350 degrees

Directions

Shake seasoning over meat. Put all ingredients into a baking dish. Turn chicken. Bake about 20-30 minutes for breasts; pieces will take 40-60 minutes.

Freezer variation: Put all ingredients into a freezer bag. Seal tight and put into freezer

1. When you ready to make this recipe, thaw in the refrigerator.

2. Preheat oven to 350 degrees.

3. Put the food into a baking dish and bake as instructed above.

Ham and Cheese Pull-Apart Biscuits

Yeah, you probably need a roasted ham. Other alternatives to bread are sliced Italian bread. Monterey cheese is a must try. This is a different take on those tasty crunchy ham and cheese sandwiches. It will be guaranteed a family thumbs up.

- 1 (16 ounce) Pillsbury Grand's Biscuits

- 1 egg

- 2 Tablespoon 2% milk

- 1 cup cheese (any kind you like)

- ¼ tsp garlic powder

- ¾ cup diced ham

Directions

1. Preheat oven to 350 degrees.

2. Grease a baking dish with olive oil or cooking spray.

3. Whisk milk and egg together in a bowl.

4. Take the biscuits and pry them open and spilt them into quarters.

5. Stir the biscuits portions into the wet mixture until it is blended.

6. Next add cheese, ham, and garlic powder.

7. Put everything into the dish and spread until the bottom is layered.

8. Bake for 25 minutes or until it golden brown.

Chapter 6 – Lighter Meals

Honey Garlic Chicken

Here a few recipes from my collection of cookbooks. This is the unfried healthier version. Do as you please with the dish. These are lower calories and they taste great, the children should enjoy it too.

- 3 T honey

- 3 lemon juice

- 3 tsp minced garlic

- 3 tsp soy sauce

- 3 chicken breasts

Directions

In Ziploc freezer bag assemble these ingredients. Put into the freezer. When you are ready to make this, thaw overnight in the refrigerator. Drizzle olive oil in a pan over low to medium flame. Add chicken and cook both sides until cooked about 20-25 minutes. Serve with cooked brown rice.

Parmesan Turkey pasta with Vegetables

Make this meal different each time. Use different pasta. Use it as a ragu. Throw some fontina cheese into the mix. A pesto recipe was mentioned and it will do well for this one too.

- 3 T olive oil

- 1 pound ground turkey

- 3 cups Broccoli florets

- 1 can Campbell's Healthy Request Cream of Celery Soup

- ½ cup sliced mushrooms

- 1 cup fat free milk

- 2 minced garlic cloves

- ½ tsp onion powder

- ½ tsp black pepper

- ½ cup parmesan cheese

Directions

1. Drizzle olive oil in a pan over medium heat. Now add the ground turkey and cook until no longer pink about 15 minutes. Add broccoli florets, soup, mushrooms, onion powder and black pepper, and parmesan cheese. Increase the temp to high to bring the food to a boil and then turn it down low. Put on a lid and simmer for 8 minutes.

2. Meanwhile cook any pasta according to package directions. Add it to the mix and serve.

3. Wait for this to cool and place in a freezer bag. Put in the freezer and when you want to make this, defrost in the refrigerator. Reheat in the microwave or on the stove until heated through.

Beef and Brown Rice
Cuts of other beef include ribeye steak, eye of round. Rinse your rice too if you don't want it sticking. You may be short on time use instant rice. Okra or tomatoes can be served too.

- 1 pound round, sirloin, or flank cut into pieces

- ¾ cup brown rice

- ½ can Healthy Request Cream of Mushroom soup

- 1 cup water

- ½ sliced mushrooms

- 1 chopped carrot

- ½ tsp Lawry's Grill Mates Steak Seasoning

Directions

1. Combine all ingredients except for rice into a freezer bag. Seal and squeeze out the air. Put into freezer. When you are ready to prepare this meal, defrost in the refrigerator overnight. Put into slow cooker and stir. Add rice. Cover it and cook on low setting 7-8 hours.

Stovetop Method; Cook brown rice. While that is cooking, drizzle a pan with olive oil over a low to medium heat and cook the meat turning once. Lower the heat to simmer and add the brown rice and simmer for 2 hours until fully heated.

London broil Chicken
A good side dish to complete this meal is penne pasta. Add cream for a simple sauce. Bowtie pasta and sun-dried tomatoes are another idea.

- 3 Tablespoons lemon juice

- Splash of red cooking wine

- 1/2 cup Worcestershire sauce

- 1 pound chicken breasts

- ½ tsp seasoning salt

Directions

1. Combine all ingredients into a zipper bag, Close and flatten to remove the air. Mix ingredients together. Put into the freezer until ready to cook. When it is time to make this dinner thaw in the refrigerator overnight drizzle olive oil in a skillet over low to medium flame. Add chicken and cook for 10 minutes.

2. Make pesto by putting 3 tablespoons toasted almonds, 3 tsp extra virgin olive oil, 2 garlic cloves or minced, 2 tsp fresh basil leaves, and a sprinkle of black pepper and nutmeg into a food processor and churn until a paste forms.

3. Spoon pesto over cooked rice. Serve.

Dijon Chicken with Parmesan Vegetables

So good it could leave you speechless. I dare you to attempt this feat. The research indicates that some households dub it, "The World's Best Chicken". Sprinkle some rosemary when it is finished. Prepare for encore requests.

- 1 pound chicken breasts
- ½ cup Dijon mustard
- 1 eggplant
- 1 zucchini
- ¼ tsp Thyme
- Parmesan cheese
- Dash of Black pepper

- Olive oil

- ½ tsp salt

Directions

1. Assemble these ingredients into a freezer bag. Flatten to squeeze out the air. Seal and put into the freezer. When you are ready to make this meal, put bag into the refrigerator to thaw overnight.

2. Preheat oven to 350 degrees. Grease a baking dish with olive oil. Sprinkle chicken and veggies with thyme and black pepper.

3. Then sprinkle with parmesan. Bake for 35 minutes. Enjoy.

Chapter 7 – More Chicken and Pork Chops

Ranch Pork Chops

<u>Brine</u> pork chops and you will be rewarded with tender, juicy meat. It is not necessary but you do can learn new things. Use salt to season the inside of the meat.

Another alternative is apple cider, apricot preserves and pan-fry them.

You are on your way to juicy pork chop goodness with this meal. It may present as assuming but give it a bit and you will see. You crock pot creates the flavor. So easy.

- 4 pork chops

- 6 medium chopped potatoes

- 2 cans cream of chicken soup

- 2 packs dry Ranch dressing mix

- 1 cup fat free milk

- ½ tsp seasoned salt

Directions

1. Coat your crock pot with cooking spray or olive oil.

2. Next put the meat on top of the potatoes.

3. Next add the soups together with the ranch dressing mix and milk. Cover the pork chops with this mixture.

4. Cook on low heat for 6-7 hours or high heat for 4 hours.

Caribbean Island Chicken

This is an island chicken recipe minus the <u>spice</u>. Great for chicken lovers and you can eat it on a regular basis. You need a big bowl to contain all the goodness detailed in this recipe. It will be a success with chicken breasts. Hot sauce and stewed red beans will have you eating well. Bold and appealing flavor.

- 1 package of Chicken cutlets

- 8 ounce can pineapple chunks, with juice

- ¼ cup packed brown sugar

- ½ tsp nutmeg

- 1/2 cup orange juice

- ½ cup raisins

- 1 splash of orange juice

-

Directions

1. Gather these ingredients. Use a Sharpie to label freezer bag with name of recipe and cooking instructions. Place on counter and fold the top over to keep it open.

2. Add chicken.

3. Pour in the rest of the ingredients.

4. Once this is done, squeeze out the air, seal, and put into the freezer.

Cooking

Thaw in the refrigerator or microwave oven. Cook on low setting in the crockpot 4-6 hours. Bake at 350 degrees for one hour.

Easy Sticky Chicken

You most likely already have them ingredients in your home. You can make wings with this recipe. It will be appreciated if they shared among a sick neighbor or someone experiencing hard times.

- 1 pack of Chicken cutlets

- 2 T olive oil

- 1 T soy sauce

- 3 T peanut butter

- 3 T ketchup

- ½ tsp salt

- ½ tsp pepper

Directions

1. Gather these ingredients. Use a Sharpie to label freezer bag with name of recipe and cooking instructions. Place on counter and fold the top over to keep it open.

2. Add chicken.

3. Pour in the rest of the ingredients.

4. Once this is done, squeeze out the air, seal, and put into the freezer.

Cooking

Thaw in the refrigerator overnight. Preheat oven to 350 degrees. Bake 40-55 minutes.

Simple Cantonese Chicken

Make this just like the restaurants and pat yourself on the back. I assume you will be preparing everything ahead of schedule. If would be nice to cook this in a wok too if you have one. Cut the chicken at a diagonal angle. Use dried black mushrooms and you can substitute steak. A honey hoisin glaze will whet the appetite. Serve with rice too.

- 1 pack of Chicken cutlets

- ¼ cup ketchup

- ¼ cup melted honey

- ¼ c soy sauce

- 2 T lemon juice

- ½ tsp Lawry's seasoned salt

Directions

1. Gather these ingredients. Use a Sharpie to label freezer bag with name of recipe and cooking instructions. Place on counter and fold the top over to keep it open.

2. Add chicken.

3. Pour in the rest of the ingredients.

4. Once this is done, squeeze out the air, seal, and put into the freezer.

Cooking

Thaw. Bake in the oven at 350 degrees for one hour or in the crockpot on low heat for 4-6 hours.

Chicken Post Haste

I know it doesn't look like much but it is still a keeper. Add some steamed rice. Great for potlucks and pork spare ribs. Mash potatoes too, for the diners who don't like rice. You need to make this a rush as the name implies. You can also double it and save yourself time.

- 1 pack Chicken cutlets

- 1/2 c ketchup

- ¼ cup water

- ¼ cup packed brown sugar

- 3 T dry onion soup mix

- ½ tsp seasoned salt

Directions

1. Gather these ingredients. Use a Sharpie to label freezer bag with name of recipe and cooking instructions. Place on counter and fold the top over to keep it open.

2. Add chicken.

3. Pour in the rest of the ingredients.

4. Once this is done, squeeze out the air, seal, and put into the freezer.

Cooking

-Thaw in the refrigerator.

-Toss in the crockpot on low heat for 4-6 hours.

Oven Method

-Preheat at 350 degrees.

-Bake for one hour and serve.

Conclusion

Do you feel better now? I hope you are relieved you can make sense of preparing meals. The busy folk can now rejoice in another task completed on the to-do list. My two are my food critics and even though I have my misses you got to keep on pushing. Never settle for the ordinary dish. The freezer is full at least for a couple of weeks. I do hope you have a new found appreciation for cooking. You are not sacrificing quality time. There is a relatively simple way to keep your family fed. Enjoy it and thanks for reading.

Dump Dinners

31 DELECTABLE MEAT & FISH DUMP DINNER RECIPES FOR EVERYONE

IMOGEN WATSON

Dump Dinners

31 Delectable Meat & Fish Dump Dinner
Recipes For Everyone

Table of content

Introduction

Dump meals may sound unattractive, but in fact they refer to meals which can be simply 'dumped' into one pan cooked and eaten. You can create surprisingly sophisticated and delicious meals this way. They are perfect for the end of a long day, or if you have guests coming and would prefer to spend your time with them, rather than slaving away in the kitchen, missing the fun.

Many of these recipes can also be prepared in advance or in double quantities, then chilled or frozen for an even quicker meal next time. Dishes which include spices and chilis are often improved by freezing or spending the night in the fridge, as this gives even more time for the flavours to infuse the dish.

None of these recipes require specialist equipment – they can all be made in a saucepan, baking tray or casserole dish. A few of them can even be made in a slow cooker – making them even more economical to cook as this is a very efficient method of preparing food.

It isn't just hearty stews that can be made into dump meals. This book also includes breakfast tray recipes (ideal for a special weekend brunch) and delicious deserts. Nor do they all rely on cuts of meat that benefit from long, slow braising – fillets of fish and joints of chicken can also be made quickly and simply. Many include carbohydrates and fresh vegetables, making then a balanced and nutritious meal.

If you are on a budget, or your time is restricted, something that will make your life easier s proper meal planning. Sit down at the start of the week and decide your family meals for the next seven days, and buy all the ingredients in a single shop. This will ensure that you have everything to hand when you need it, as well as reducing food waste. For example, if you know you are making a meal which includes fresh herbs, choose another one with the same herbs for later in the week, so you can be sure a big bunch will not go to waste. This is cheaper than shopping on a daily basis, and means that you are not left with odds and ends of ingredients which cannot be made into a single dish.

However, it is important not to become a slave to your meal plan – if you find that you do not fancy a particular meal on any given night, simply swap it in for another later in the week. You can always have a 'picnic day' on the morning before your next shop, when you eat up any leftovers from the week.

Chapter 1 – Cheese and Chicken Casserole

This is a great way to use up roast chicken from a Sunday lunch

<u>You will need:</u>

3-4 chicken breasts, cooked and chopped into bite sized pieces (approximately 350g)

400g of egg noodles or pasta, cooked

250 ml of sour cream

2 x 400g cans of cream of chicken soup

200g grated cheddar cheese

200g grated mozzarella cheese

1 sleeve of Ritz crackers, crushed into chunks (not to a powder)

75g butter or margarine, melted

2 Tablespoons of poppy seeds (optional)

Method:

Mix together the chicken, canned soup, both sorts of cheeses and the sour cream, then when completely combined, add the noodles. Tip into an oven-proof dish.

Heat the butter in the microwave until melted and mix together with the crackers to form a topping. Spread over the top of the dish and sprinkle with poppy seeds, if using.

Bake at 180 degrees for thirty minutes until the top in crispy and the cheese has melted.

Chapter 2 – Beef Stroganoff

A classic Russian dish

<u>You will need:</u>

1 kg of stewing beef, cut into bit sized pieces (you can cook this from frozen of you desire)

200g of Mushrooms, sliced or quartered

1 packet of onion soup mix

1 small can of Cream of Mushroom Soup

1 can of Ginger Ale (do not use diet or reduced calorie versions)

1 heaped tablespoon of corn starch

200ml of sour cream

Slow cooker

<u>Method:</u>

Place frozen stew meat in the slow cooker with the soup and soup mix, mushrooms and ginger ale. Cook for 5 hours on high (or overnight on low).

Mix the corn flour with a little cold water and add to the mix one hour before the end of cooking time. Stir in the sour cream just before serving the stroganoff over pasta or traditional noodles.

Chapter 3 – Cowboy Chicken

This tasty dish has a delicious smoky flavour from the paprika

<u>You will need:</u>

4 skinless chicken breasts

1 small can of sweet corn

1 x 400g of black beans

2 x 400g can of chopped tomatoes

Half a teaspoon each of smoked paprika, mixed herbs and ground black pepper

One red chilli, chopped (adjust this to personal taste)

<u>Method:</u>

Place all ingredients into your pressure cooker and cook on high for six hours or until the chicken is cooked through.

Serve with rice or flatbreads if desired, although the beans make this dish tasty and filling all by itself.

Chapter 4 – Deep Dish American Style Pizza

A far cry from the crisp, wafer thin bases found in Italy, but none the less delicious for that!

<u>You will need:</u>

1 can of American-style savory biscuit dough

300g of marinara sauce

Pizza toppings of your choice – Pepperoni, sliced onions, olives, sweetcorn, etc

350g mozzarella cheese, grated

<u>Method:</u>

Lightly grease an oven proof casserole dish, and line with the biscuit mix. Spread over the marinara sauce and cover with the toppings of your choice. Scatter over the cheese and bake in the oven at 180 degrees for 30 minutes or until the base is cooked.

Chapter 5 – One Dish Pasta Bolognese

The pasta and sauce cook together, ensuring that the flavours penetrate the pasta itself – as well as saving on the washing up!

<u>You will need:</u>

500g of minced beef – choose a lower fat steak mince
1 large jar of marina sauce

Pasta shapes of your choosing – you will need the same volume as the jar of sauce

200g ricotta cheese

200g mozzarella cheese

A teaspoon each of dried oregano, basil and parsley

Fresh basil to serve (optional)

<u>Method:</u>

In a large, deep sided frying pan, cook the beef, stirring to break up the mince until the beef is cooked through. Add the marinara sauce, then fill the empty jar with water and tip that into the pan. Finally, fill the jar with dried pasta and add to the pan along with the dried herbs.

Cover and cook for ten minutes, then uncover and check the pasta. If it is still not cooked and the mixture looks dry, add a little more water. When the pasta is still al dente, stir through the cheeses and serve.

Chapter 6 – Asparagus Breakfast Tray

A luxurious weekend brunch treat – serve in bed for extra decadence

<u>You will need:</u>

6 slices of streaky smoked bacon

10 asparagus spears

A small bunch of fresh thyme and parsley

salt and pepper

4 large eggs

<u>Method:</u>

Rinse and trim the asparagus spears. Lay the bacon slices on the bottom of a baking sheet and place in the oven at 180 degrees until crispy.

When the bacon is cooked, move the slices to a warmed plate, and roll the spears in the bacon fat to coat. Put the spears in the oven for a few minutes until they start to soften, then arrange them together in two groups of five. Crack two eggs over each group of spears, season, and cook until the whites are set. Serve with the crispy bacon.

Chapter 7 – Maple Mustard Chicken with Wedges

Tangy mustard and sweet maple syrup make this sticky chicken irresistible

<u>You will need:</u>

4 chicken thighs, skin on and bone in

750g of potatoes

Salt and pepper

1 tablespoon of cider vinegar

A splash of white wine (option)

1 tablespoon of wholegrain mustard

Olive oil

<u>Method:</u>

Mix together all the ingredients except the chicken and potatoes in a large bowl or ziplock bag. Add the chicken thighs and leave to marinade for 15 minutes.

Scrub the potatoes and cut into wedges. Preheat the oven to 180 degrees, then drizzle the wedges in a little more olive oil and cook for 15 minutes.

Remove the chicken from the marinade and add to the potatoes, skin side up. Roast for thirty minutes or until the chicken is cooked through.

Chapter 8 – Fennel and Pork Chops

The mild aniseed flavour of the soft fennel works perfectly with the oven-crisp pork

<u>You will need:</u>

4 pork loin chops (one per person)

2 baking potatoes, cut into chunks or wedges

1 red pepper, sliced and deseeded

4 cloves of garlic

1 fennel bulb, cut into wedges

300ml stock – vegetable or chicken

1 Tablespoon of tomato puree

A small bunch of thyme, leaves stripped

<u>Method:</u>

Preheat the oven to 180 degrees. In a large roasting tin, mix the potato, fennel, red pepper, thyme and garlic (do not remove the sin from the cloves) and spread out into an even layer. Combine the stock with the tomato paste and pour over the vegetables. Add to the pan, cover with foil and roast for half an hour.

After the time has elapsed, turn up the heat to 220 degrees and add the chops on top of the vegetables. Cook for a further 20 minutes – the pork should be crisp and golden brown.

Chapter 9 – Sticky Peanut Chicken

A classic combination of Asian flavours in minutes

<u>You will need:</u>

2 chicken breasts, skins removed

2 tablespoons of vegetable oil

3 Tablespoons each of tomato ketchup and crunchy peanut butter

1 Tablespoons of light soy saucepan

<u>Method:</u>

Mix together all ingredients in a ziplock bag and add the chicken breasts. Leave to marinate for fifteen minutes, then place each breast in a aluminium parcel. Place each parcel on a baking sheet and cook in the oven for half an hour. After this time, open the parcels and allow the breast to continue cooking for a further fifteen minutes or until cooked through.

Chapter 10 – Pork And Rice

This recipe keeps the lean tenderloin soft and moist without drying out in the oven

<u>You will need:</u>

1 Whole pork tenderloin, trimmed of excess fat and sinew and sliced

1 medium onion, sliced

Half a cooking chorizo (about 75g) skinned and cut into wedges

150g long grain rice

100g of green beans

2 peppers (red, green or yellow) sliced and deseeded

Salt and pepper

750ml of stock – chicken or vegetable

1 teaspoon each of cumin, chili powder and coriander

2 tablespoons of olive oil

2 cloves of garlic, chopped

Method:

In a large frying pan, heat the oil and soften the onions until they are golden. Season both ides of the pork slices with salt and pepper, then add to the pan and brown for a few minutes, then add the garlic, chorizo, beans and peppers. Add the spices, fry together for three minutes.

Pour over the stock and add the rice, and bring to the boil. Reduce to a simmer and cook for 20 minutes until the rice is cooked and the liquid has been absorbed.

Chapter 11 – Crispy Vegetable Gratin

A satisfying main course for vegetarians and meat-eaters alike

<u>You will need:</u>

1 medium yellow squash

1 onion, thinly sliced

2 ripe tomatoes

1 medium baking potato

75g parmesan cheese

A few sprigs of fresh thyme

Salt and pepper

Olive oil

<u>Method:</u>

Preheat oven to 180 degrees. Scrub and de-eye the potato, then slice it and all the other vegetables (except the onion) into rounds a quarter of an inch thick.

Thinly slice the onion and fry in a little oil over a medium heat until it softens. Spread the onions over the bottom of an over proof dish, then arrange the sliced vegetables on overlapping layers on top. Sprinkle with the parmesan and thyme and season, then cover with foil and cook for half an hour. Remove the foil and continue to cook for a further 30 minutes until the potato is cooked through.

Chapter 12 – Wasabi Salmon

The firm, oily flavour of the salmon stands up to the fiery wasabi, and the bok choi retains its crunch throughout the cooking process

<u>You will need:</u>

4 salmon fillets, skins removed

1 teaspoon of wasabi paste

Fresh ginger, peeled and grated – start with a piece the same size as your thumb

2 cloves of garlic, chopped

Salt and pepper

2 or 3 heads of bok choy, halved

A handful of finely shredded savoy cabbage – about 125g

100g mushrooms – chestnut or shiitake, sliced

Olive oil

1 tablespoon of mayonnaise

Method:

Preheat the oven to 180 degrees and put a baking sheet in there to heat up.

Season the salmon fillets on both sides and lay each on a large piece of foil. Toss the mushrooms, cabbage and bok choy with a drizzle of olive oil and the ginger and garlic. Divide the vegetables between the four salmon fillets and scrunch over the foil to make a sealed package. Roast on the baking sheet for ten minutes, then open up the package to release the steam for the last five minutes of cooking time.

Meanwhile, mix the mayonnaise and wasabi together and serve with the salmon and vegetables for dipping.

Chapter 13 – Squash, Lentil and Bean Stew

Another delicious vegetarian recipe for everyone to enjoy.

<u>You will need:</u>

1 small butternut squash, peeled and cut into chunks

100g red lentils

1 onion, thinly sliced

1 x 400g chopped tinned tomatoes

1 x 400g kidney beans

2 teaspoons of dark brown sugar

A splash of red wine vinegar

2 teaspoons of ground cumin

Half a teaspoon of chili flakes (adjust to taste)

Olive oil for frying

Fresh parsley to serve

Method:

In a saucepan, heat a little oil and fry the onion and squash for a few minutes until the squash begins to soften. Add the cumin and chilli and cook for one minute to release the oils. Tip in the tomatoes and fill the empty can with water and add along with the lentils, vinegar and sugar. Bring to the boil then reduce to a simmer and cook for 10 minutes. Add the beans and cook for a further five minutes or until the lentils are tender.

Chapter 14 – Quick Paella

Okay, so it's not a classic paella, but the flavours of the chorizo give this dish a deep, rich, authentic flavour.

<u>You will need:</u>

200g raw prawns

50g cooking chorizo

1 onion, peeled and sliced

2 peppers, sliced and deseeded (you can choose red, green or yellow)

250g easy cook rice

1 x 400g chopped tomatoes

2 cloves of garlic

Olive oil for frying

Method:

Fry the onion in a little olive oil, then add the peppers, chorizo and garlic. Cook for another three minutes, then ti[in the tomatoes and 500ml of recently boiled water. Stir in the rice, cover and bring back to the boil, then cook for 12 minutes. Uncover and check the rice has not stuck to the bottom – it should be firm but not fully cooked. Add the prawns and a little more water if the mixture looks dry. Cook, stirring frequently, until the prawns are cooed through. Season to taste.

Chapter 15 – Parmesan Chicken with Roasted Romaine

The great crunch of the parmesan brings this whole dish together. Add anchovies as well for added depth == unless you really can't stand them!

<u>You will need:</u>

4 skinless, boneless chicken breasts

2 large hearts of romaine, halved lengthwise

Salt and pepper

75g of grated Parmesan cheese

75g of panko breadcrumbs

3 tablespoons of olive oil

A small bunch of flat-leaf parsley

2 garlic cloves, peeled and finely chopped

4 anchovy fillets (optional)

1 lemon, cut into wedges, to serve

<u>Method:</u>

Preheat the oven to 180 degrees. Line a large rimmed baking sheet with foil or baking parchment.

Place the chicken between two sheets of clingfilm and bash with a saucepan or rolling pin to flatten. Season the chicken on both sides with salt and pepper and place on the baking sheet. Mix together together the parmesan, breadcrumbs, 2 tablespoons of the olive oil, half of the garlic and the parsley. Carefully pat the crust onto one side of the breasts and roast for fifteen minutes in the oven.

While you are waiting for the chicken to cook, drizzle the cut sides of the romaine lettuce with the remaining oil and rub over the other half of the garlic. Season with salt and pepper. Place around the chicken and return to the oven.

When the chicken is cooked through and the lettuce has begun to blacken at the edges, divide the anchovies between the lettuces and return to the oven for a few minutes. Serve with the lemon wedges.

Chapter 16 – Pot Roast Pork

This gorgeous roast pro recipe is ideal for sandwiches the next day – that is, if there's any left over!

<u>You will need:</u>

1kg joint of pork, boned and rolled

2 onions sliced

4 leeks, trimmed, washed and cut into three parts each

2 cloves of garlic

A large glass of white wine

Sunflower oil for frying

25g of butter

6 bay leaves

A small bunch of fresh thyme, or a teaspoon of dried thyme

5 crushed juniper berries

1 Tablespoon of white wine vinegar

1 Teaspoon of caster sugar

Method:

Preheat the oven to 180 degrees. Unroll the pork joint and lay the bay leaves, half of the thyme and the garlic over it/ Re-roll the joint and tie it with butcher's string.

In a casserole dish heat the oil and butter and brown all sides of the pork. Add in the onions and soften for a few minutes. Add the sugar, vinegar and juniper berries and stir in, then add the leeks, wine and the remaining thyme, cover and cook in the oven for two hours until the meat is tender.

Chapter 17 – Caribbean Chicken

Another quick recipe that draws on classic flavours to give the chicken real depth and excitement.

You will need:

3 skinless chicken breasts

1 x 400g of pineapple chunks in syrup

1 heaped tablespoon of dark brown sugar

1 heaped tablespoon of golden raisins

1 teaspoon of nutmeg

1 red chili, finely chopped (optional)

Method:

Preheat the oven to 180 degrees.

Cut the chicken into bite sized pieces and mix together with all the other ingredients in an oven proof dish.

Bake for 45 minutes, stirring occasionally. The juice should all evaporate and the chicken become dark and sticky.

Chapter 18 – Pomegranate Chicken

Don't be scared of pomegranate – the best way to get the seeds out is to cut the fruit in half, turn it over and bash on the skin with a spoon. The seeds will tumble out, perfectly separated.

You will need:

6 chicken joints – thighs or drumsticks

2 sliced onions

4 cloves of garlic sliced

300ml tomato passata or jar of tomato sauce

1 teaspoon of paprika

1 red chilli, finely sliced (adjust for desired heat)

A small bunch of fresh coriander, chopped

200ml pure pomegranate juice

The seeds of one pomegranate

Olive oil

Salt and pepper

1 pack of precooked white rice

Method:

Brown the chicken joints in the olive oil over a medium heat. Season with salt, pepper and paprika and cook for ten minutes. Remove to a plate.

In the same pan cook the onions, scraping at any residue from the chicken on the bottom of the pan. Add the garlic, chili, coriander, passata and pomegranate juice and bring to the boil.

Return the chicken to the pan and simmer for 30 minutes until the chicken is cooked through. Garnish with the fresh pomegranate seeds and serve with the rice.

Chapter 19 – Classic Lemon Chicken

<u>You will need:</u>

2 skinless chicken breasts

3 cloves of garlic, crushed and chopped

Olive oil

A small bunch of fresh chopped parsley

The juice of one lemon

Salt and pepper

<u>Method:</u>

Combine all the ingredients in a bowl or ziplock bag and marinade the chicken breasts for a minimum of fifteen minutes and up to four hours.

Remove the breasts and place on a baking tray and roast for forty five minutes, or until the chicken is cooked through.

Chapter 20 – Peach Cobbler

Who said puddings have to take time? This delicious cake can even be knocked up between courses.

<u>You will need:</u>

2 x 400g cans of peaches in sweetened syrup

100g self raising flour

100g caster sugar

100g butter

1 egg

1/2 a teaspoon of ground cinnamon

<u>Method:</u>

Preheat your oven to 180 degrees. Empty the peaches into the bottom of a 9×13 pan – if the peaches are halved, you may want to cut them into smaller pieces.

Mix together the dry ingredients with the egg and spread the batter over the peaches. Cut the butter into small chunks and distribute evenly over the batter. Bake for 45 minutes (reduce to 30 minutes if using a fan assisted oven).

Chapter 21 – Cherry Betty

<u>You will need:</u>

2 400g cans of cherry pie filling

100g self raising flour

100g caster sugar

200g butter

1 egg

200g pecans

2 teaspoons of cinnamon

<u>Method:</u>

Preheat your oven to 180 degrees. Lightly grease a 9×13 baking tin and line with baking parchment.

Pour both cans of cherry pie filling into the bottom of the baking tin. Mix together the flour, sugar and cinnamon with a beaten egg and spread over the cherries. Add the pecan pieces – you can use whole, halved or chopped pecans, depending on what you have to hand.

Put the butter in a small dish and microwave to melt. Pour over the melted butter but do not mix in. Bake for 30 minutes.

Chapter 22 – Pumpkin Pie

An ideal recipe for Halloween

<u>You will need:</u>

1 x 400g of canned pumpkin

1 small can of sweetened evaporated milk

3 eggs

½ A teaspoon each of cinnamon, allspice and nutmeg

100g self raising flour

100g caster sugar

200g of chopped pecan nuts

<u>Method:</u>

Grease and line a 9 inch cake tin and preheat the oven to 180 degrees.

Combine all ingredients except the pecan nuts and the butter and beat well together. Tip into the prepared tin, but do not smooth the top. Melt the butter for a few seconds in the microwave and tip over the mixture then sprinkle on the pecan nuts.

Bake for 45 minutes and check the centre with a skewer – it this does not come out clean, cook for a further 5 minutes and check again.

Chapter 23 – World's Simplest Chocolate Cake

You will need:

1 egg

100g of unsweetened cocoa powder (not drinking chocolate)

300g plain flour

200g caster sugar

100ml of hot water

100g of butter or margarine

100ml of buttermilk

1 teaspoon of baking soda

A pinch of salt

Chocolate chips (optional)

Method:

Grease and line a deep side square baking tray.

Mix all ingredients together thoroughly and pour into the tin. Scatter over the chocolate chips if using. Bake at 180 degrees for 30 minutes.

Chapter 24 – Easy Moussaka

<u>You will need:</u>

1 x 425g tinned lamb mince

300g frozen ratatouile

250g ricotta cheese

300g lasagne cheese sauce

2 Tablespoons of tomato puree

Salt and pepper

A splash of red wine

A teasoon each of cinnamon and nutmeg

A small bunch of chopped mint

1 tablespoon of parmesan

<u>Method:</u>

Combine the tomato purée, red wine, mint and cinnamon with the tin of lamb and the ratatouille and season.

Mix the ricotta cheese, eggs and cheese sauce together, add the nutmeg and some salt and pepper.

Tip half of the meat mixture into a baking dish and spoon over a third of the cheese sauce. Add the rest of the meat, top with all the cheese sauce and sprinkle on the parmesan. Bake at 180 degrees for half an hour until the top is golden brown.

Chapter 25 – Spinach Egg Hash

<u>You will need:</u>

400g new potatoes, cut into bite sized pieces

75g butter

1 onion, sliced

A large handful of fresh spinach leaves, washed

Salt and pepper

8 eggs

1 red pepper, sliced and deseeded

chili flakes (optional)

1 Tablespoon of parmesan

Parsley to serve

<u>Method</u>

In a deep sides frying pan, add the potatoes with enough water to cover and boil rapidly for ten minutes until the potatoes are tender. If there is any remaining water, drain it off. Add the butter and cook the onions and peppers amongst the potatoes for five minutes until they soften, then scatter the chili flakes (if using). Add the spinach and allow it to wilt, then make four wells in the pan. Crack two eggs into each well and turn down the heat. Cover the pan and cook for five minutes or until the whites are set but the yolks are still runny. Scatter with parmesan and parsley to serve.

Chapter 26 – Filling Corn Chowder

<u>You will need:</u>

300g frozen sweet corn

1 onion, diced

50g butter

3 large floury potatoes

500ml of chicken or vegetable stock

2 bay leaves

A bunch of leafy green vegetable – kale, savoy cabbage or spinach, chopped

100g strong cheddar cheese

1 teaspoon of cumin seeds

Salt and pepper

1 tablespoon of plain flour

250ml whole milk (or half milk and half cream)

<u>Method:</u>

Cook the onion in the butter over medium heat in the bottom of a large saucepan. When the onion has softened, add the cumin seed, stock, potatoes, bay leaves and green vegetables. Bring to the boil reduce to a simmer and cook for around 20 minutes until the potatoes are tender.

Add the frozen corn to the soup. Combine the flour with the milk and add to the soup to thicken. Add the cheese before serving and season with black pepper.

Chapter 27 – Prawn and Artichoke

You will need:

500g of large prawns, shelled and deveined

1 x 400g of canned, drained artichoke hearts, cut into quarters

3 ripe tomatoes, diced

2 cloves of garlic, chopped

Salt and pepper

1 tablespoon of olive oil

A small bunch of chopped parsley

Half a teaspoon of paprika

Chili flakes (optional, to taste)

Method:

In a large non-stick pan, heat the olive oil and chili flakes, and coo for a few minutes. Add the garlic, cook for another minute, then add the remaining ingredients. Stir constantly until the prawn is cooked through.

Chapter 28 – Turkey and Broccoli Bake

<u>You will need:</u>

750g tenderstem broccoli

400g cooked turkey meat

75g butter

1 onion, sliced

6 mushrooms, sliced

3 Tablespoons plain flour

500ml stock – vegetable or chicken

2 Tablespoons of white wine or dry sherry

A splash of double cream (optional)

1 Tablespoon of grated parmesan

Sliced almonds to garnish

<u>Method:</u>

In a deep lined baking tray, arrange the broccoli in a single layer, then dot over with butter. Top with the sliced onions and turkey meat, sprinkle with flour and then arrange the sliced mushrooms. Pour in the stock and wine, season and cover tightly with foil. Cook at 180 degrees for 30 minutes, then remove the foil Top with the parmesan and continue to cook until the top is crispy. Serve with a swirl of cream and almonds to garnish.

Chapter 29 – Potato, Bacon and Rosemary Pizza-Style Flatbread

<u>You will need:</u>

Prebought pizza dough base

100g fontina cheese (or any other good melting cheese with a strong flavour)

2 sprigs of fresh rosemary, leaves stripped and finely chopped

250g new potatoes, washed and thinly sliced (use a mandolin is possible)

4 rashers of cooked streaky bacon

1 Tablespoon of Parmesan cheese, grated

<u>Method:</u>

Arrange the sliced fontina cheese on the pizza base, then sprinkle with the rosemary.
Arrange the sliced potato in an even layer and crumble the bacon over the top. Bake at 200 degrees until the base is crispy.

Chapter 30 – Greek Style Lamb Meatballs

<u>You will need:</u>

250g lean lamb mince

50g white breadcrumbs – do not use panko

2 baking potatoes, cut into six wedges each

2 courgettes, sliced lengthways into batons

A dozen cherry tomatoes, or another small variety

1 beaten egg

2 onions, peeled and cut in half

A bunch of fresh mint, chopped and stalks removed

50g feta cheese

Olive oil

Salt and pepper

<u>Method:</u>

Preheat the oven to 180 degrees. Mix together the lamb mince, egg, half of the chopped mint, half a grated onion and seasoning then form into eight small balls. Cut the remaining onion into wedges and arrange on a baking tray along with the potatoes, courgettes, tomatoes and lamb patties. Drizzle with olive oil, season and bake in the oven for around 40 minutes. Serve scattered with crumbled feta and the remaining mint.

Chapter 31 – Sausage Stew

<u>You will need:</u>

6 thick sausages

1 x 400g tin of tomatoes

100g of pitted black olives

500g sliced mushrooms – button or chestnut

200ml stock

2 cloves of garlic, sliced

1 teaspoon of dried oregano

Vegetable oil for frying

<u>Method</u>

Cut the sausages into one inch chunks and fry in a little oil for five minutes until browned on all sides. Add the garlic and oregano, cook for one minute and add the stock, mushrooms, olives and tomatoes.

Simmer for fifteen minutes until the sausages are cooked through and the sauce has thickened.

Conclusion

We hope you have enjoyed this guide to Dump Cooking. Whether you have a saucepan, baking tray or casserole dish, there's always something tasty and surprising that you can whip up in a few minutes.

28871160R00078